Hearing

Lillian Wright

Watts Books
London • New York • Sydney

© 1994 Watts Books

Watts Books
96 Leonard Street
London EC2A 4RH

Franklin Watts Australia
14 Mars Road
Lane Cove
NSW 2060

UK ISBN: 0 7496 1205 3

Design: Sally Boothroyd
Artwork: Mainline Design
Cover artwork: Jonathan Gill

A CIP catalogue record for this book
is available from the British Library

Dewey Decimal Classification 612.8

Printed in Italy by G. Canale & SpA

Contents

What is hearing?

We are able to hear many sounds if our ears are working properly. We can hear very soft sounds, like a fly buzzing. We can hear very loud sounds, like an aeroplane flying overhead. When we listen, we can discover things about the world around us. Listening can tell us about things we may not be able to see.

▽ Hearing is one of our five senses.

Looking at our ears

We have two ears at the side of our head which we use to detect sounds. Only the soft, outer part of the ear can be seen. The rest is protected by our bony skull. This is because it is very delicate. Sounds are made by air vibrating, or moving to and fro.

▷ Our ears let us hear someone else talking.

▽ Sound waves can't be seen, but travel through the air to our ears.

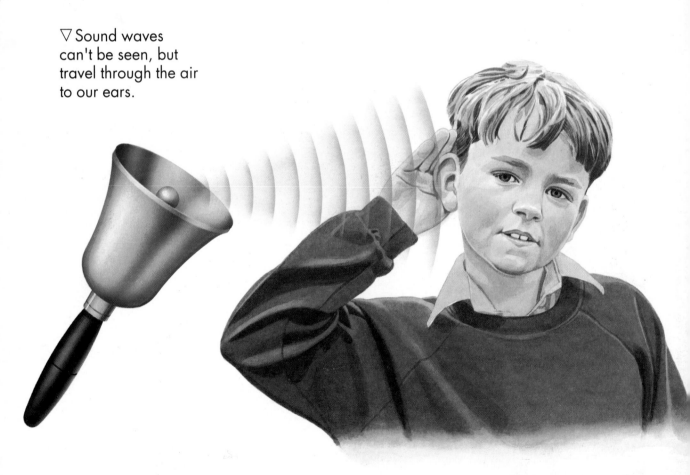

Our ears are different

Our ears vary in shape and size. The shape of our ear is inherited. This means they are like our parents' ears. Some people have large lobes at the bottom of their ears. Others have none at all. Some people can waggle their ears. Most humans cannot move their ears, though. Many animals can.

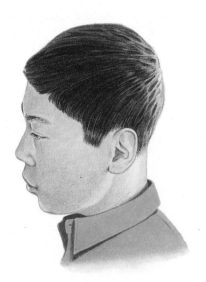

▷ Rabbits have long ears at the top of their heads which they can move in the direction the sound is coming from.

△ Our ears come in all shapes and sizes.

6

How do we hear?

The outer part of our ears is used to 'catch' sounds. Sounds usually reach our ears by travelling through the air as sound waves. They pass along the ear canal to the eardrum. This vibrates and makes the middle ear and the inner ear vibrate. Messages travel to the brain along the **auditory nerve**. Our brain tells us what we are hearing.

▽ Sounds 'beat' our eardrums like a musician playing a drum.

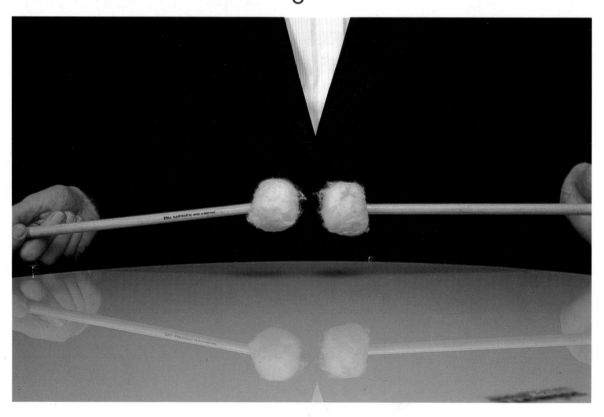

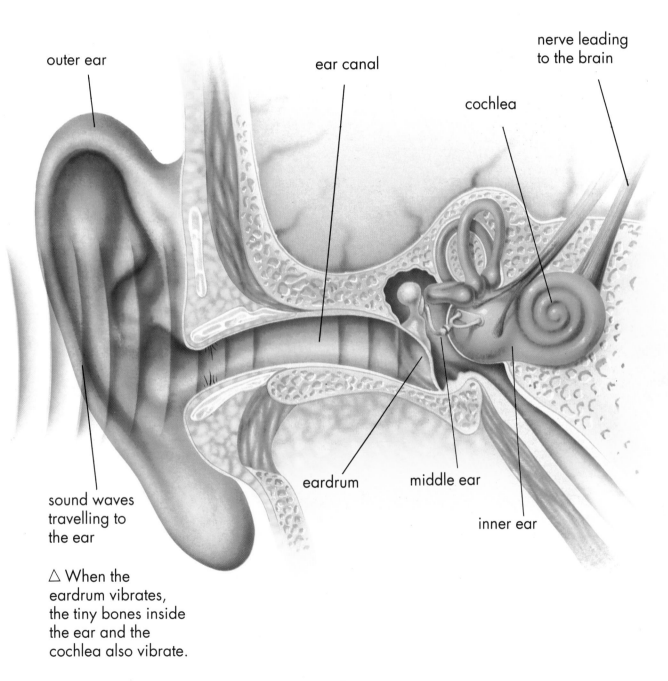

outer ear

ear canal

nerve leading
to the brain

cochlea

sound waves
travelling to
the ear

eardrum

middle ear

inner ear

△ When the
eardrum vibrates,
the tiny bones inside
the ear and the
cochlea also vibrate.

Hearing sounds

Sounds travel through the air at about 340 m every second. Quiet sounds travel just as quickly as loud sounds, but do not go as far. Sounds can travel faster through liquids like water and solids like wood or metal than they do through the air. To hear all the sounds being made around us, the sound waves have to reach our eardrum and start it vibrating.

▷ The sound of the referee's whistle travels through the air to the ears of the football player.

▽ The tap sounds louder when the child has his ear on the desk, because sound travels better through a solid than through the air.

Listening carefully

Our ears can hear loud and soft sounds. Sometimes we have to move closer to a very soft sound to hear it. A doctor may use a stethoscope so that she can hear our breathing or heartbeat. Some sounds are so loud that our ears can hear them even when we are far away. Many animals can hear sounds that we cannot.

▽ A whale can hear very low sounds over hundreds of miles.

▷ A bat can hear
very high sounds.

▽ A doctor can hear
someone's quiet
heartbeat using
special instrument
called a
stethoscope.

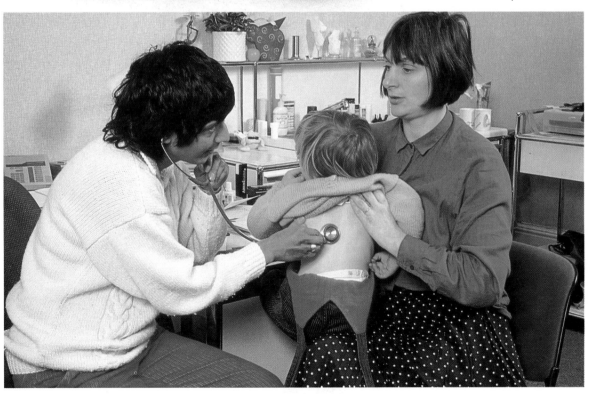

How well can you hear?

Some people can hear better than others. But this is not because they have better ears. They may listen more carefully. A doctor or nurse checks children at school in case they have something wrong with their ears. Someone may be able to hear better with one ear than with the other. Some people can hear high sounds better than low ones. Quiet sounds may be difficult to hear.

▷ People called audiometricians can check to see if we can hear high and low sounds properly using special machines.

▽ We whisper when we don't want others to hear us.

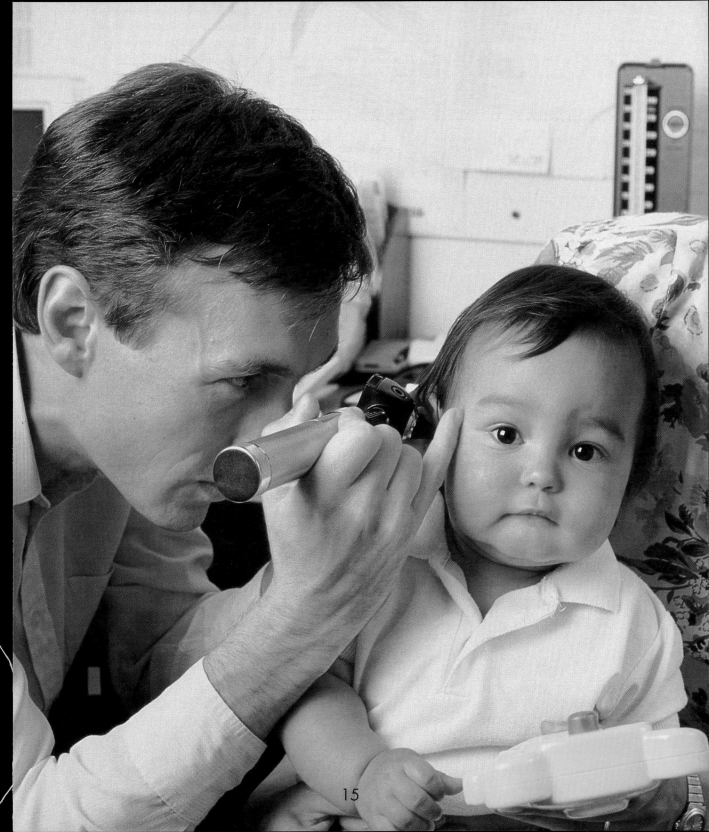

Recognising sounds

▷ We usually hear our own name being called.

Sometimes we can hear quiet sounds that we know very well, like our own name being called. We learn to recognise many sounds, even if they reach our ears at the same time. If there are a lot of sounds around us, we may not be able to hear what we want. If we are not listening, the sounds may reach our ears, but are not 'heard' by our brain.

▷ Sometimes we don't want to hear the sounds that reach our ears!

▷ On the telephone
we may not always
recognise who is
speaking.

Why have two ears?

Our two ears are at the side of our head to let us hear sounds from all around. If we hear someone calling for help we know which way to run to get to them. Animals that have their ears at the front of their heads can move them about. This lets them know exactly where any sound is coming from.

▽ If we can't see where a sound is coming from, our two ears will tell us.

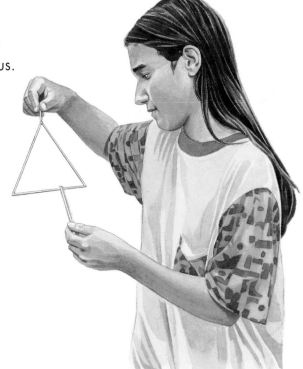

▷ This child's ear nearest the window hears the other person's voice calling first.

▽ Listening for a sound of danger coming from any direction is important for a deer's survival.

Ear care

We need to look after our ears so that we can hear clearly. We need to wash them so that they do not get too dirty. We must not put anything inside our ears because that could damage them or stop us hearing properly. Even loud noises can hurt or damage our ears.

▷ People who work with noisy machines wear ear-muffs to protect their ears from the very loud sounds.

◁ Sticky yellow wax in the outer ear and ear canal traps dirt and dust and stops it entering our ears.

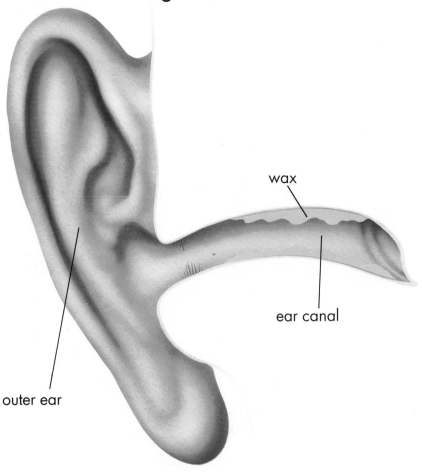

wax

ear canal

outer ear

Hearing loss

Some people cannot hear clearly. This may be because of an accident or illness. Some babies are born with ears that do not work very well. Hearing aids can help these people to hear more. Deaf and partly deaf people may use their hands to 'talk'. This is called signing. Some also learn to tell what others are saying by watching their lips.

▽ Hearing aids are usually electronic devices which are designed to pick up sounds and make them louder.

▽These children are talking together using sign language.

▷Subtitles on the television help deaf people enjoy the programmes they cannot hear.

Enjoying listening

As well as loud and soft sounds, we can hear high and low sounds. Musical instruments can make all sorts of different sounds – the beat of a drum or the toot of a trumpet. Music is a mix of sounds that we can enjoy. Most people around the world listen to songs and music. They can be recorded on to cassette tapes or compact discs for everybody to enjoy.

▷ We can recognise many different musical instruments playing at the same time, such as an orchestra.

▽ Tape recorders and televisions let us listen to all sorts of sounds and music.

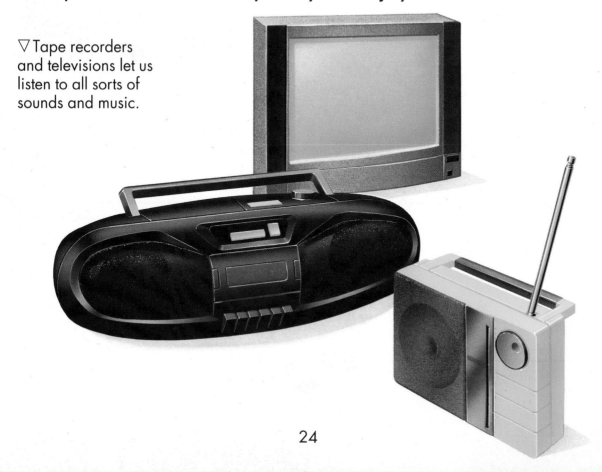

Noise pollution

Sounds that we do not want to listen to can be very annoying. Many machines that we use make noises that we don't want. Aeroplanes and cars help us to travel but are very noisy. All unwanted noise is called noise pollution. Some machines can be made quieter.

▷Life in cities is usually very noisy. How many noise-makers can you see in this picture?

▷The silencer on this motorbike helps to cut down noise.

Hearing from afar

If we want to hear something better we can go closer to the source of the noise. Sometimes it is not possible to do this, and so machines have been invented to help us. A megaphone, a personal radio and a telephone are all inventions that make our voice sound louder at a distance. Sometimes a sound bounces back by itself to give an **echo**.

▷ Telephones allow us to speak to people thousands of miles away.

▷ The person's shout travels back from the cliff face to give an echo.

Things to do

- Tap a table top with your finger. Then listen again with your ear on the table top. What do you notice?

- Collect as many pictures of animal ears as possible. Compare them with your own ears.

- Think about how you can help to reduce noise pollution. Do you always listen to music very loud? Do you really need to?

Glossary

auditory nerve The nerve which goes from the ear to the brain.

cochlea The bony structure inside the ear which converts sound waves into electrical signals which pass along the auditory nerve to the brain.

ear drum The thin, skinlike layer that is stretched across the entrance to the middle ear. It vibrates when sound waves hit it.

echo A repeated sound. An echo is heard when a sound bounces back from a distant hill or wall so that you hear it again.

hearing aid A device to make sounds louder and help those who are hard of hearing hear better.

megaphone A funnel-shaped instrument used to increase the sound of a voice.

signing Movements of the hands which stand for words and ideas and form a language that people who cannot hear well can use.

stethoscope An instrument used to hear sounds produced in the lungs, heart or other parts of the body.

vibrating Moving rapidly back and forth.

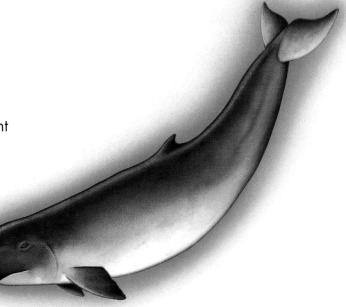

Index